First Biographies

Bessie Coleman

by Eric Braun

Consulting Editor: Gail Saunders-Smith, PhD
Consultant: Lynne Byrd Spivey, Director
The Atlanta Historical Museum

Mankato, Minnesota

Pebble Books are published by Capstone Press,
151 Good Counsel Drive, P.O. Box 669, Mankato, Minnesota 56002.
www.capstonepress.com

1 2 3 4 5 6 10 09 08 07 06 05

Library of Congress Cataloging-in-Publication Data
Braun, Eric, 1971–
    Bessie Coleman / by Eric Braun.
    p. cm.—(Pebble Books. First biographies)
    Includes bibliographical references and index.
    ISBN 0-7368-4229-2 (hardcover)
    1. Coleman, Bessie, 1892–1926—Juvenile literature. 2. African American women
air pilots—Biography—Juvenile literature. 3. Air pilots—United States—Biography—
Juvenile literature. I. Title. II. Series: First biographies (Mankato, Minn.)
TL540.C546B75 2006
629.13'092—dc22   2004028520

Summary: Simple text and photographs present the life of Bessie Coleman and how
she became the first African American woman to earn a pilot's license.

Note to Parents and Teachers

The First Biographies set supports national history standards for
units on people and culture. This book describes and illustrates the
life of Bessie Coleman. The images support early readers in
understanding the text. The repetition of words and phrases helps
early readers learn new words. This book also introduces early
readers to subject-specific vocabulary words, which are defined in
the Glossary section. Early readers may need assistance to read
some words and to use the Table of Contents, Glossary, Read More,
Internet Sites, and Index sections of the book.

Table of Contents

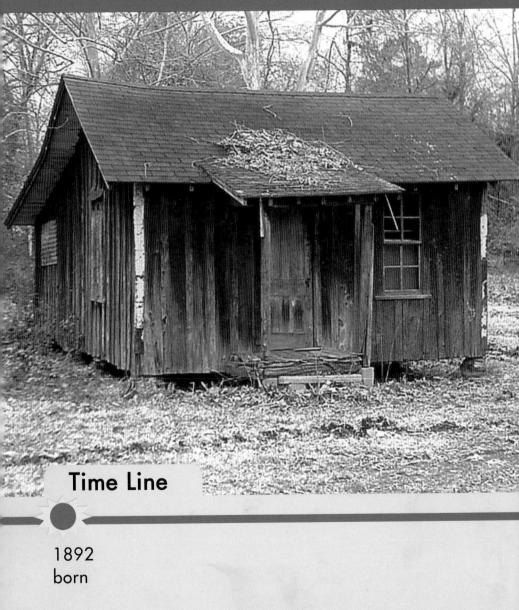

Time Line

1892
born

Young Bessie

Bessie Coleman was born
in Texas in 1892.
She had 12 brothers
and sisters. Her family lived
in a one-room cabin.

◀ Bessie's family lived in a small cabin like this one.

Time Line

1892
born

Bessie had to work hard when she was very young. Her family was poor and needed money. Bessie picked cotton and washed clothes. She did not like these jobs.

◀ people picking cotton around 1900

Time Line

1892
born

1910
goes to
college

Bessie dreamed of doing something more exciting.
At age 18, Bessie went to college. She read about pilots and airplanes. Bessie decided she wanted to be a pilot.

the first airplane flight in 1903

Time Line

1892
born

1910
goes to
college

Learning to Fly

Most pilots were men. Only a few white women could fly. American schools would not teach black women to fly. But Bessie wanted to go to flight school anyway.

an American flight school around 1919

Time Line

1892
born

1910
goes to
college

1920
leaves for
France

Bessie learned that most female pilots lived in France. In 1920, she found a flight school in France that would teach her to fly. Bessie's dreams were coming true.

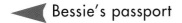 Bessie's passport

Time Line

| 1892 born | 1910 goes to college | 1920 leaves for France | 1921 earns pilot's license |

Bessie earned her pilot's license in 1921. She was the first black woman in the world to earn a pilot's license. Bessie went back to the United States to start flying.

Bessie around 1921; Bessie's pilot's license (inset)

Time Line

1892 born	1910 goes to college	1920 leaves for France	1921 earns pilot's license

Stunt Flier

In 1922, Bessie began flying in air shows. Her small airplanes were open to the sky. She did daring stunts. People loved to watch her fly. They called her "Queen Bess."

1922
begins flying
in air shows

Time Line

| 1892 born | 1910 goes to college | 1920 leaves for France | 1921 earns pilot's license |

Bessie remembered the hard jobs she did as a child. She wanted to help other black people learn to fly. She hoped to open a flight school for them.

◄ Bessie (right) with a friend around 1924

1922
begins flying
in air shows

Time Line

1892
born

1910
goes to
college

1920
leaves for
France

1921
earns pilot's
license

Bessie died in an airplane accident in 1926. She never opened her flight school. But a flight school was named for Bessie in 1929. Her life still inspires people today.

the Bessie Coleman Aero Club in 1930

1922
begins flying
in air shows

1926
dies in airplane
accident

1929
Bessie Coleman
Aero Club opens

Glossary

air show—an event where pilots display their flying skills

cabin—a small, roughly built house

college—a school students attend after high school

cotton—fluffy, white fibers used to make cloth

France—a country in Western Europe

inspire—to give someone the idea to do something

pilot—a person who flies airplanes

pilot's license—a piece of paper that gives a person permission to fly airplanes

stunts—difficult tricks

Read More

Brager, Bruce L. *Bessie Coleman*. New York: Scholastic, 2002.

Hart, Philip S. *Bessie Coleman*. Just the Facts Biographies. Minneapolis: Lerner, 2005.

Walker, Sally M. *Bessie Coleman: Daring to Fly*. On My Own Biography. Minneapolis: Carolrhoda Books, 2003.

Internet Sites

FactHound offers a safe, fun way to find Internet sites related to this book. All of the sites on FactHound have been researched by our staff.

Here's how:

1. Visit *www.facthound.com*

2. Type in this special code **0736842292** for age-appropriate sites. Or enter a search word related to this book for a more general search.

3. Click on the **Fetch It** button.

FactHound will fetch the best sites for you!

Index

Word Count: 257
Grades: 1–2
Early-Intervention Level: 18

Editorial Credits
Aaron Sautter, editor; Heather Kindseth, set designer; Patrick D. Dentinger, book designer; Kelly Garvin, photo researcher / photo editor

Photo Credits
Corbis / Underwood & Underwood, cover
Courtesy of Atlanta Historical Museum / Steven Smith, 4
Courtesy of Special Collections and Archives, Wright State University, 8
Getty Images Inc. / Hulton Archive / O. Pierre Havens, 6
Smithsonian National Air and Space Museum, 1, 10, 12, 14 (both), 16, 18, 20

TM 2005 Family of Bessie Coleman by CMG Worldwide, Inc. / www.CMGWorldwide.com